(my name)

loves to ____________________

____________________.

This is a drawing of what I love to do.

AF584320

My progress chart

As you complete each page, find the letter here. Trace the letter and draw a picture.

mM
nN
oO
pP
qQ
rR
sS
tT
uU
vV
wW
xX
yY
zZ

Continue the patterns. Keep your pencil on the page.

Copy the patterns.

Handwriting: clockwise fluency patterns.

Continue the patterns. Keep your pencil on the page.

Copy the picture.

Handwriting: anticlockwise fluency patterns.

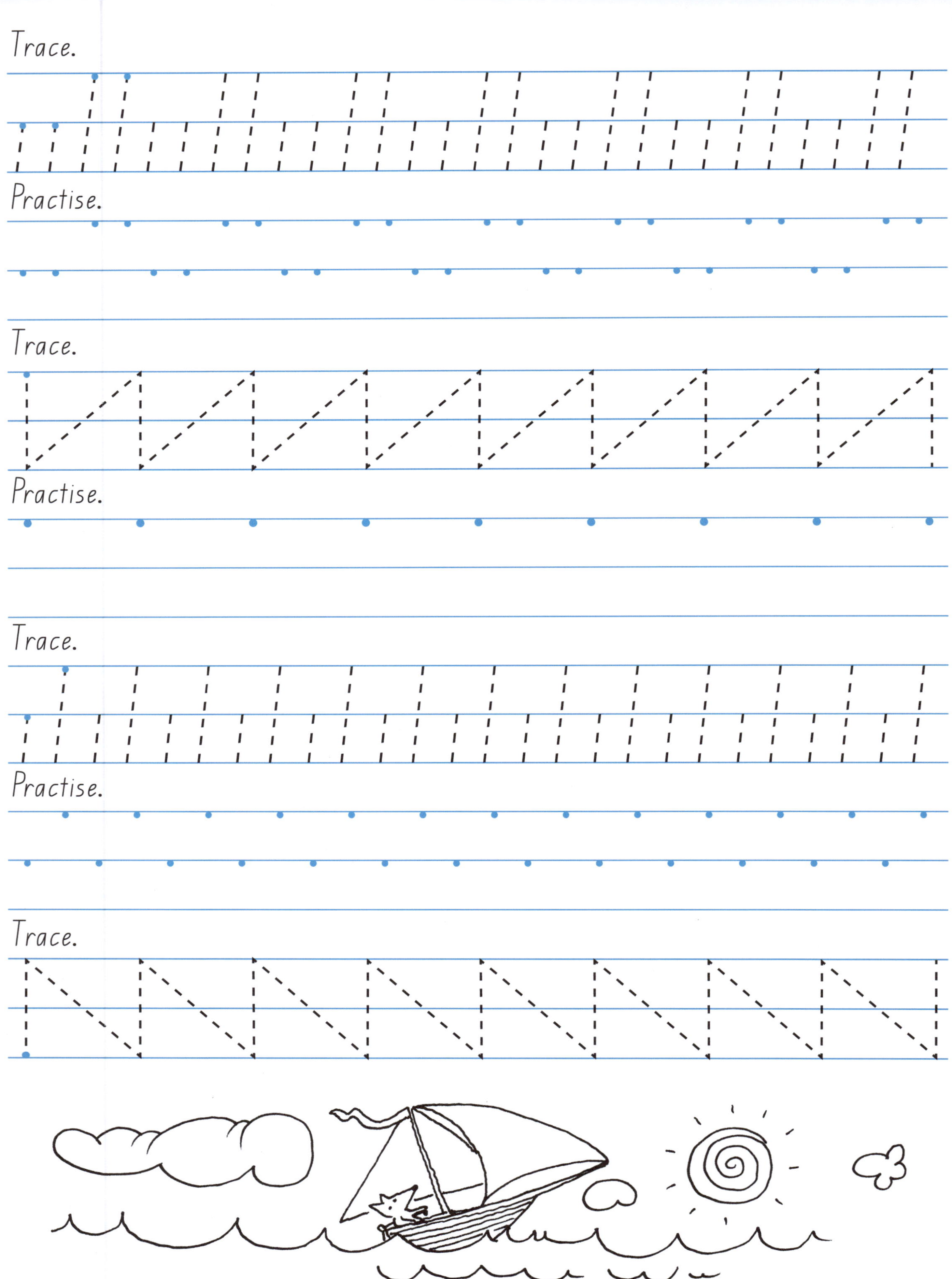

Handwriting: linear fluency patterns and downstroke.

Copy the patterns. Start at the dots.

Handwriting: patterns.

Handwriting: clockwise letter; body letter (m).
Grammar: simple sentence; action verb (munch); adjectives (merry, messy); nouns (monkeys, melons).
Punctuation: upper-case (capital) letter to start a sentence; full stop.
Spelling and vocabulary: mad, March, May, melon, meow, merry, mess, messy, Monday, monkey, monster, moo, mother, mud, mum, munch.
Literary elements: alliteration.

Trace then write.

M M M

m

M

Trace then write.

Merry monkeys munch

on messy melons.

Rate your writing

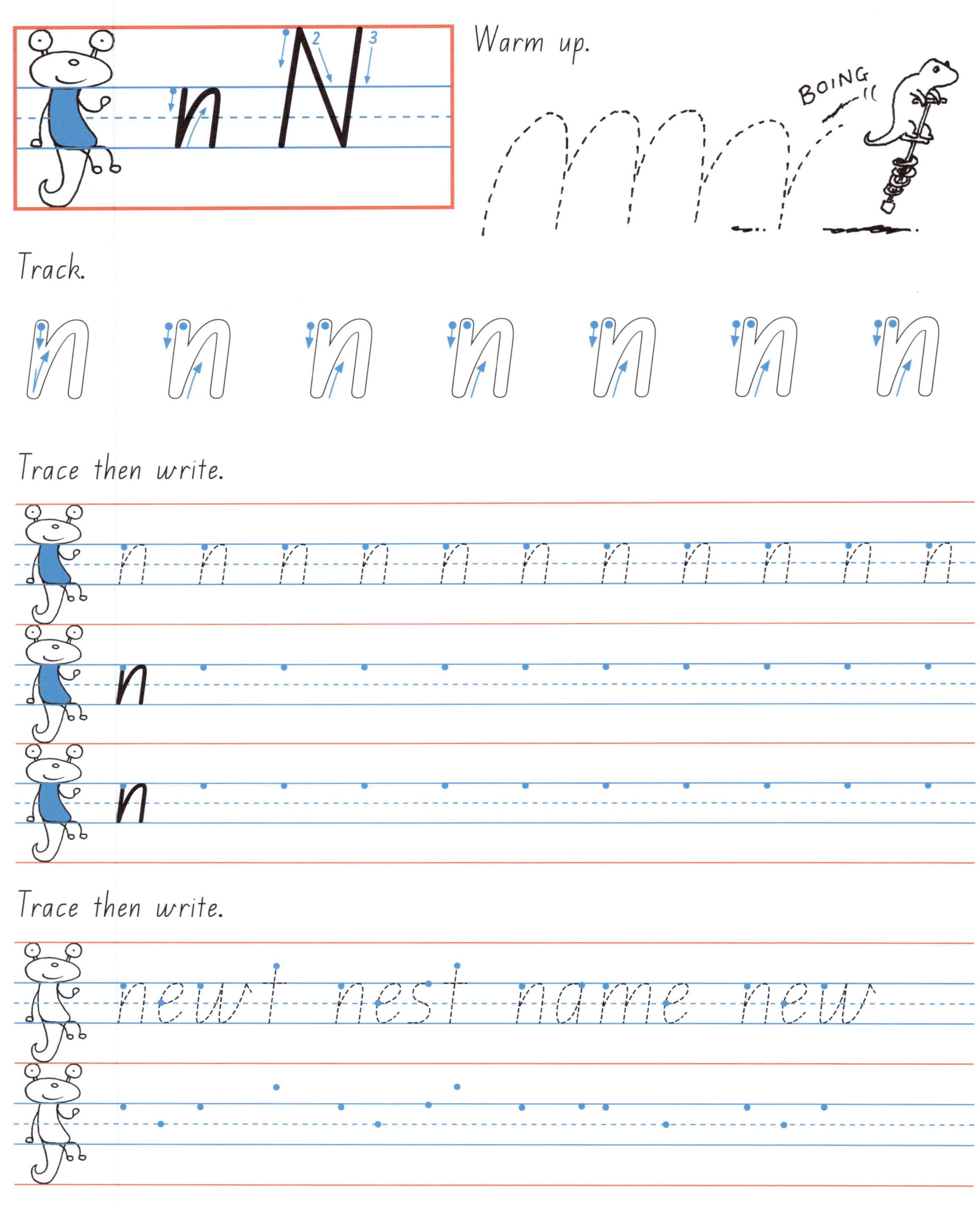

Handwriting: clockwise letter; body letter (n).
Grammar: simple sentence; adverb (noisily); action verb (nibbled); proper noun (Nonna, Nina); common noun (noodles).
Punctuation: upper-case (capital) letter to start a sentence; full stop; apostrophe for possession (Nina's).
Spelling and vocabulary: name, nest, new, newt, next, nibble, nice, nine, no, noodles, not, never, Nonna, November, now.
Literary elements: alliteration.

Trace then write.

N N N

n

N

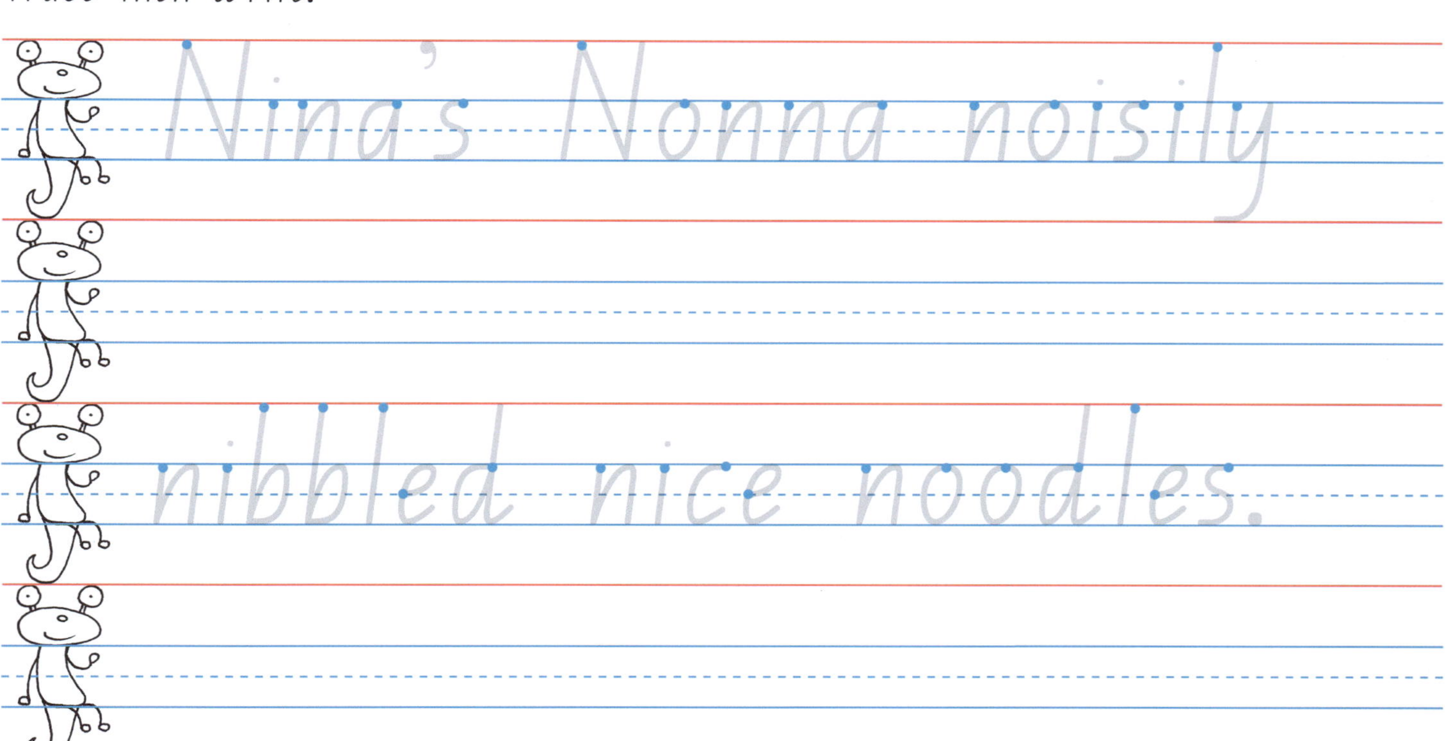

Trace then write.

Nina's Nonna noisily

nibbled nice noodles.

Handwriting: clockwise letter; head and body letter (ascender) (h).
Grammar: quoted speech; being verb (are); saying verb (shouted); adjective (hungry); exclamation; question.
Punctuation: upper-case (capital) letter to start a sentence; exclamation mark; quotation marks; question mark.
Spelling and vocabulary: hair, hang, hawk, help, hen, hid, hide, hiss, hum, hog, home, honey, hospital, how, howl, hungry, heart.
Literary elements: alliteration; onomatopoeia (hiss, howl); folk tale (Hansel and Gretel).

Trace then write.

H H H

h

H

Trace then write.

"Hello! How are you?"

shouted hungry Hansel.

Rate your writing

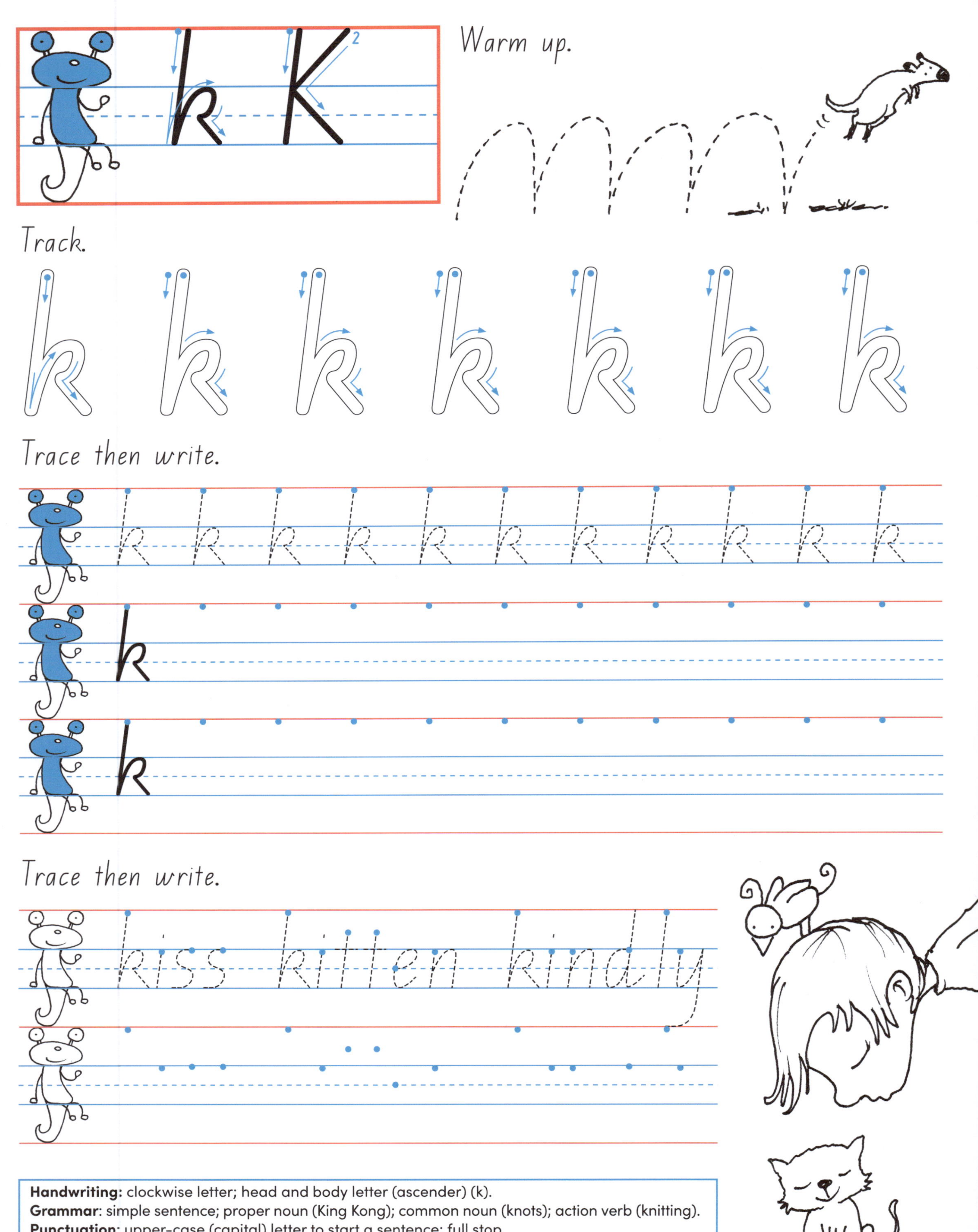

Handwriting: clockwise letter; head and body letter (ascender) (k).
Grammar: simple sentence; proper noun (King Kong); common noun (knots); action verb (knitting).
Punctuation: upper-case (capital) letter to start a sentence; full stop.
Spelling and vocabulary: key, kind, kiss, kitten, koala; silent k (knee, knew, knit, knots, know).
Literary elements: alliteration; story character (King Kong); anthropomorphism.

Trace then write.

K K K

k

K

Clickity clack

Trace then write.

King Kong knew he

kept knitting knots.

Rate your writing

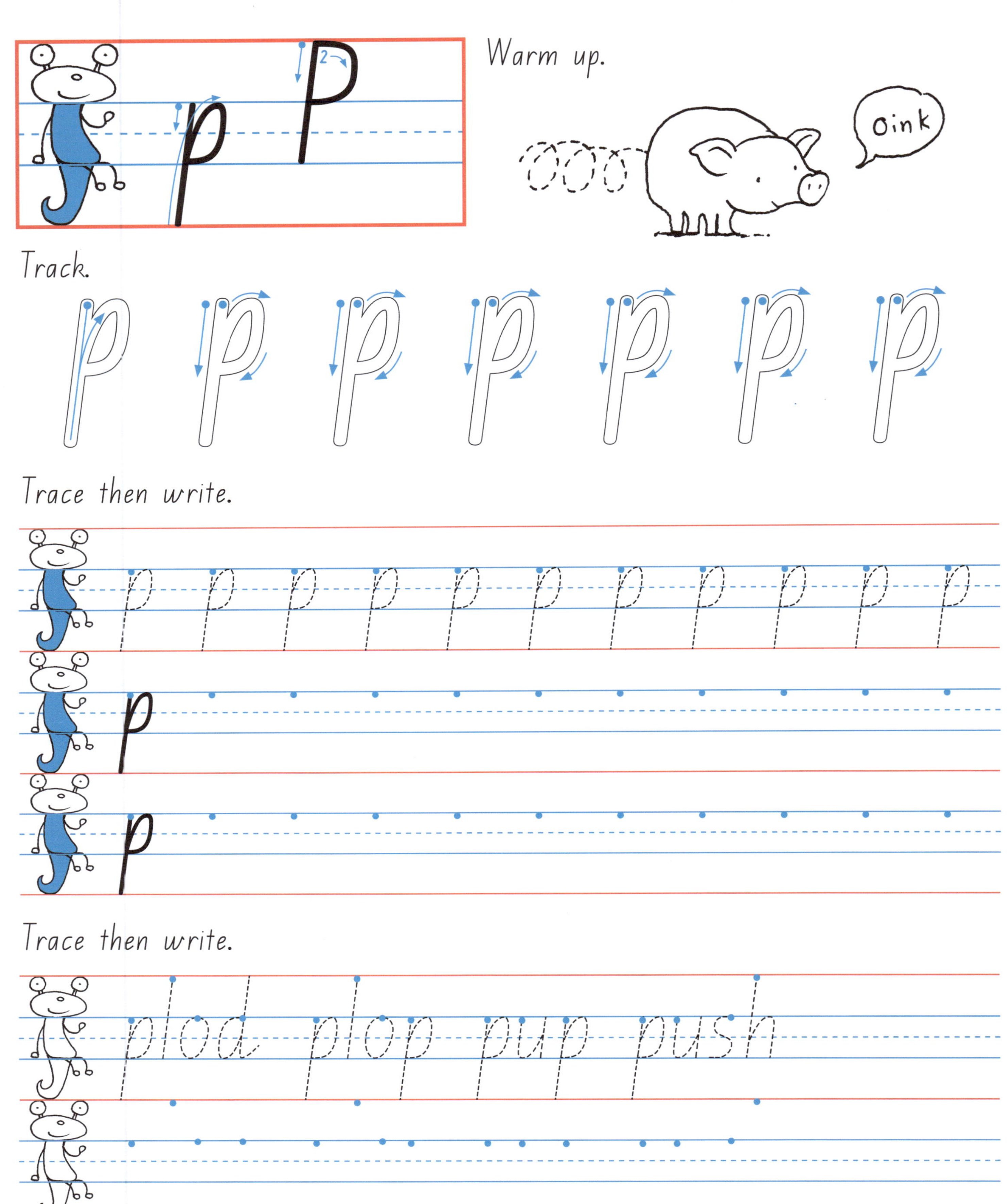

Handwriting: clockwise letter; body and tail letter (descender) (p).
Grammar: simple sentence; action verbs (poked, plod); proper noun (Pedro); common noun (python ; article (a).
Punctuation: upper-case (capital) letter to start a sentence; full stop.
Spelling and vocabulary: peep, pet, pencil, pig, pimple, pink, plop, plus, poke, pong, pony, possum, post, pumpkin, push, put, python.
Literary elements: alliteration; onomatopoeia (plop).

Trace then write.

P P P

p

P

Trace then write.

Pedro poked and

pushed a python.

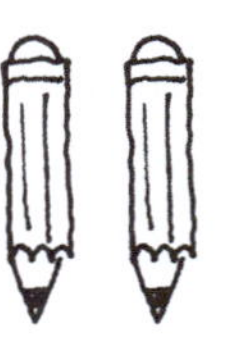

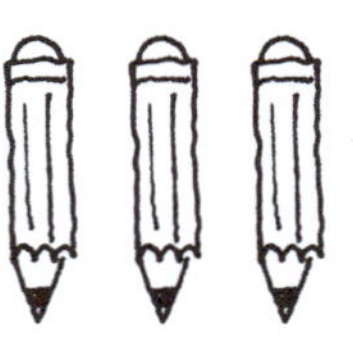

Handwriting: clockwise letter; head and body letter (ascender) (b). **Grammar**: simple sentence; action verb (boogied); nouns (bunyips, band); noun group (a bush band). **Punctuation**: upper-case (capital) letter to start a sentence; full stop.
Spelling and vocabulary: baby, bag, banana, band, bear, before, best, better, big, bird, boat, book, boom, brag, bring, brown, burp, bush, bunyip. The word *bunyip* is from the Wathawurung and Dharug languages.
Literary elements: alliteration; onomatopoeia (beep, boom); anthropomorphism.

Trace then write.

B B B

b

B

Trace then write.

Bunyips boogied in a

bush band.

Rate your writing

Handwriting: clockwise letter; body letter (r).
Grammar: simple sentence; adjectives (red, rude); proper noun (Roger); common noun (robot); noun group (the rude red robot).
Punctuation: upper-case (capital) letter to start a sentence; full stop.
Spelling and vocabulary: rabbit, raft, ran, rang, rat, read, red, real, reeks, ring, roast, robot, rot, rude, run, rush, rushing.
Literary elements: alliteration.

Trace then write.

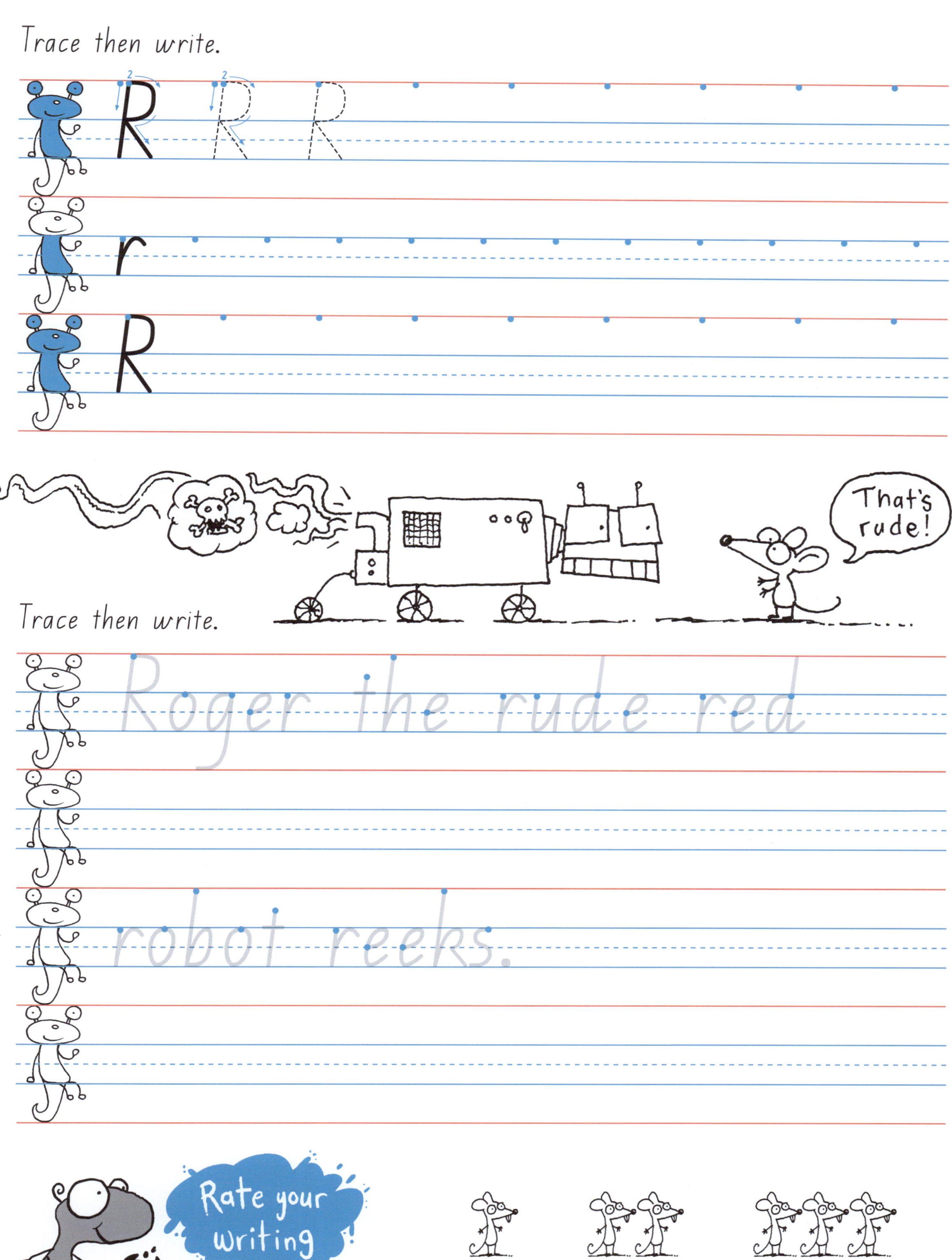

Trace then write.

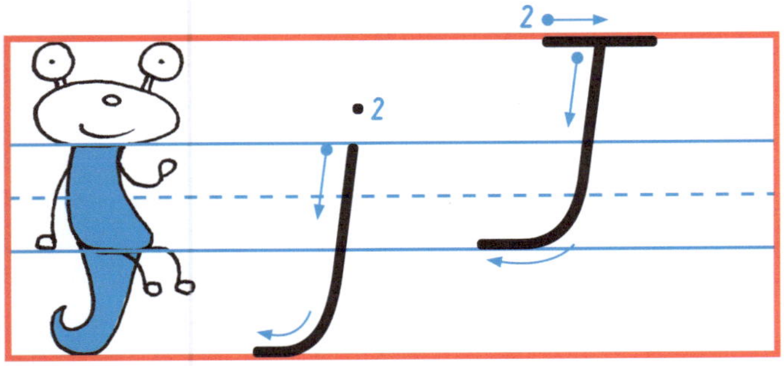

Warm up.

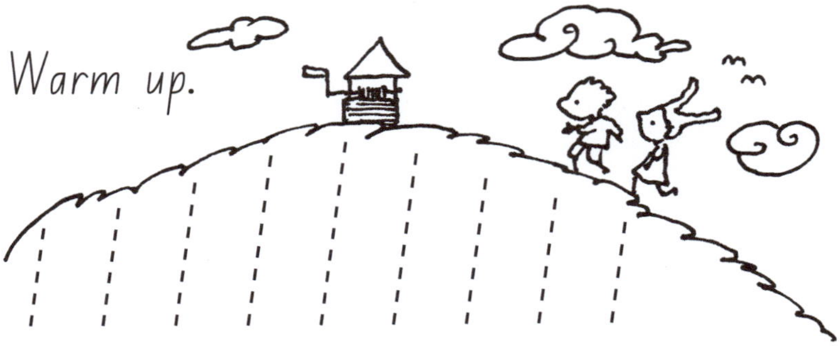

Track.

Trace then write.

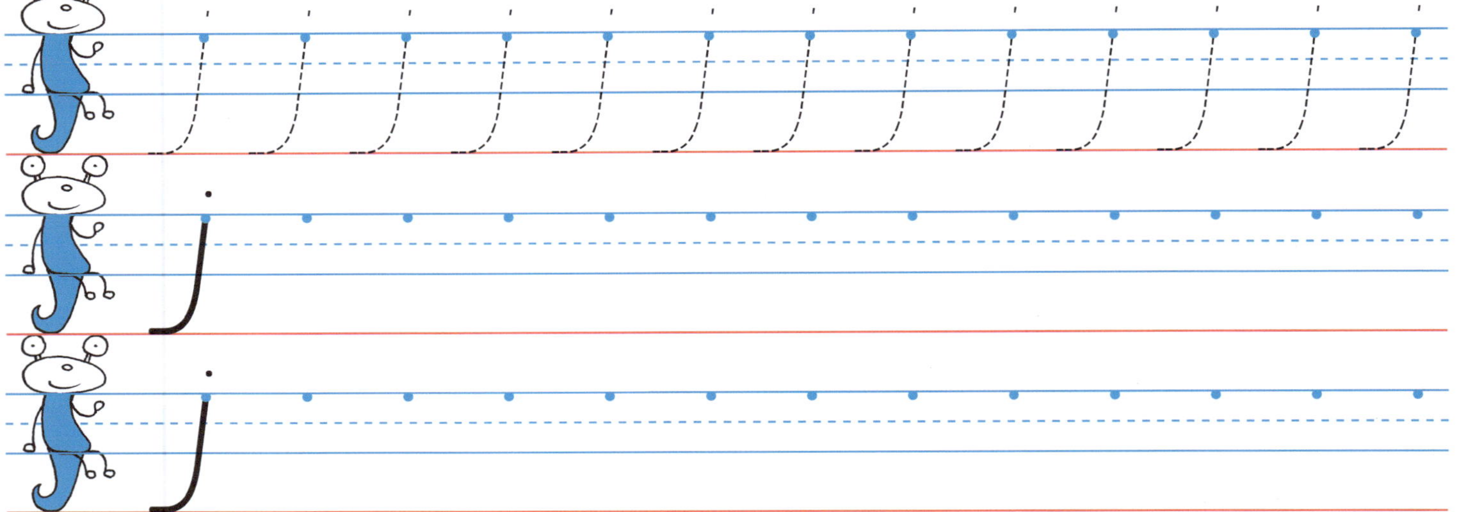

Trace then write.

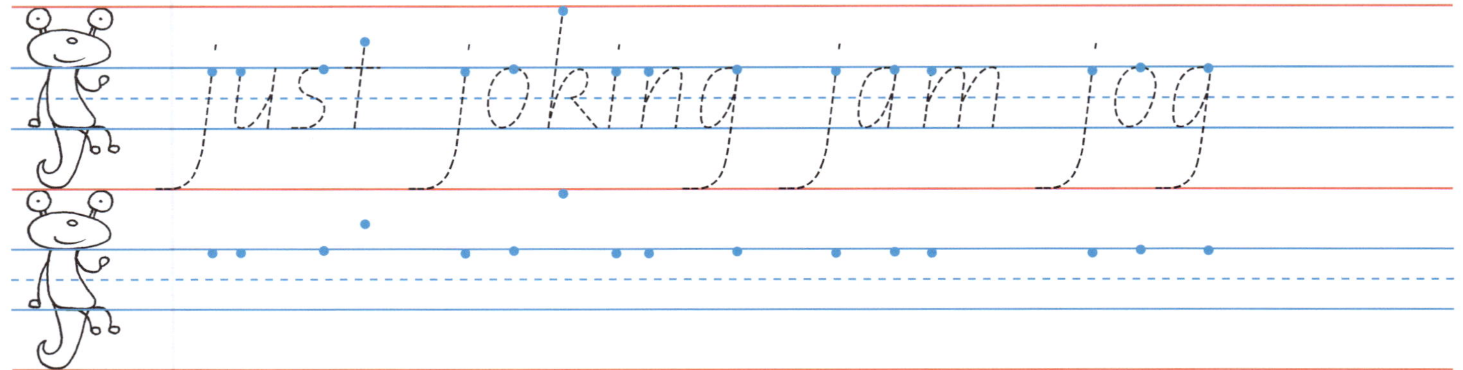

Handwriting: clockwise letter; body and tail letter (descender) (j).
Grammar: simple sentence; action verbs (jiggles, jumps, jogs); proper noun (Jill).
Punctuation: upper-case (capital) letter to start a sentence; full stop.
Spelling and vocabulary: jagged, jam, jammed, January, jet, jelly bean, jiggle, joey, jog, join, joke, July, June, jumps, just.
Literary elements: alliteration; nursery rhyme (Jack and Jill).

Trace then write.

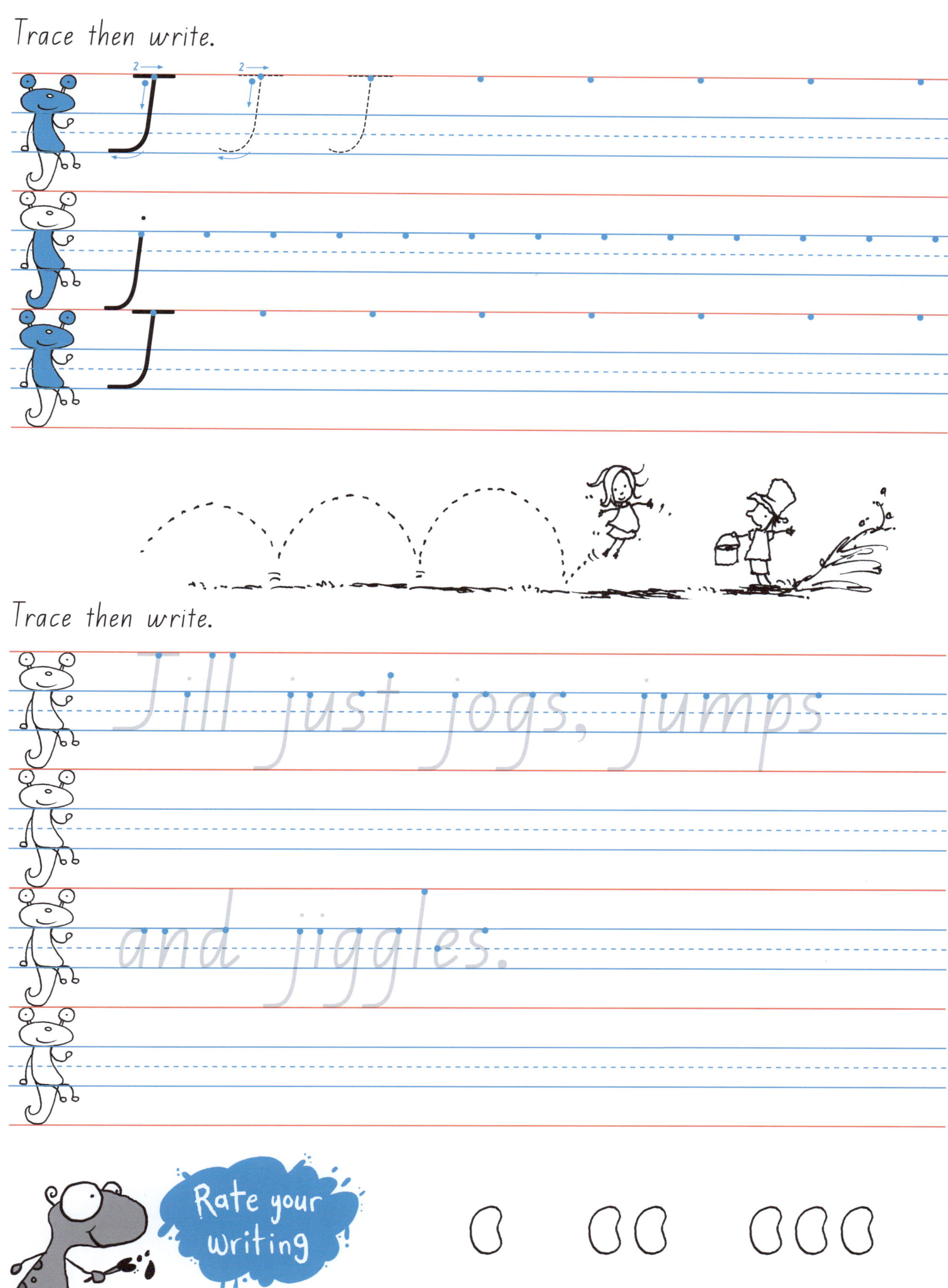

Trace then write.

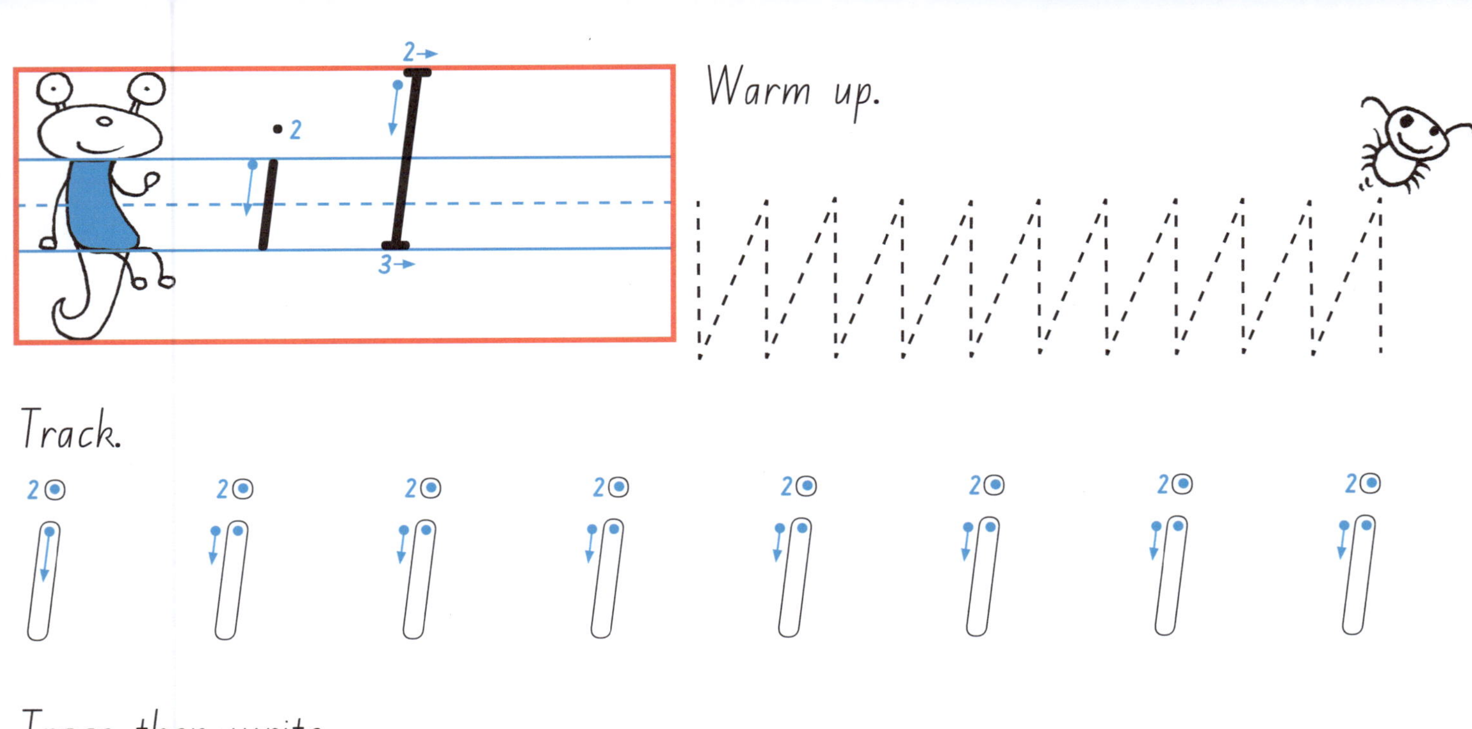

Track.

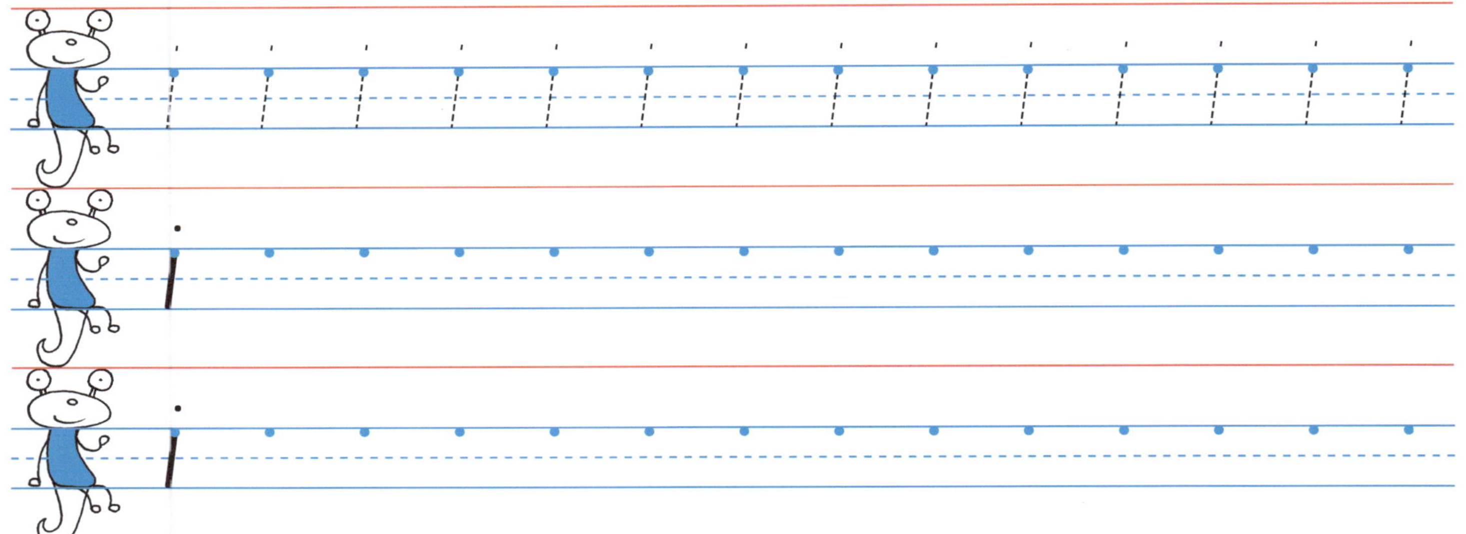

Trace then write.

Trace then write.

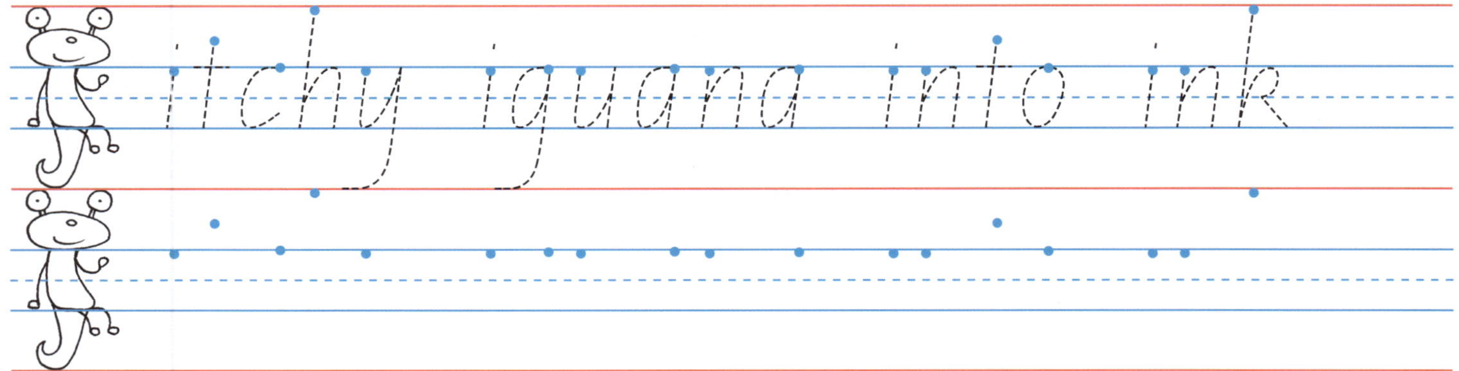

Handwriting: straight-line letter; body letter (i).
Grammar: simple sentence; proper noun (Iggy); adjective (itchy); being verb (is); prepositional phrase (in bed).
Punctuation: upper-case (capital) letter to start a sentence; full stop.
Spelling and vocabulary: icky, idea, idol, igloo, iguana, imp, in, ink, insect, inside, into, is, isn't, it, itchy.
Literary elements: alliteration.

Trace then write.

Trace then write.

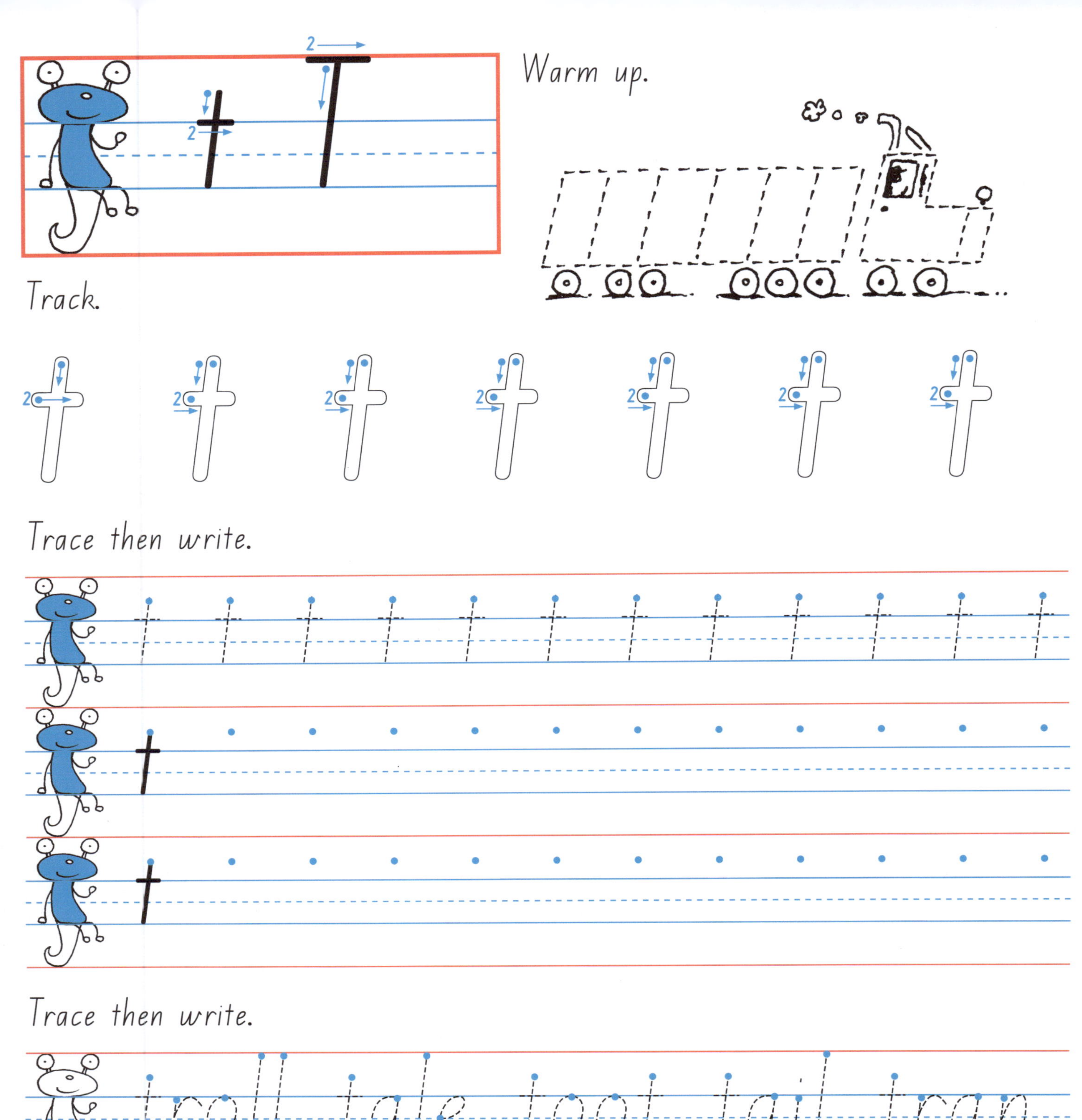

Handwriting: straight-line letter; head and body letter (ascender) (t).
Grammar: simple sentence; possessive (its); nouns (turtle, time); adjective (timid); noun group (the timid turtle).
Punctuation: upper-case (capital) letter to start a sentence; full stop.
Spelling and vocabulary: tail, tale, take, Tuesday, Thursday, time, timid, took, toot, tooth, trap, troll, try, turtle, ten, twelve, two.
Literary elements: alliteration; story character (troll); onomatopoeia (toot, tick-tock); play on words (took its time).

Trace then write.

Trace then write.

The timid turtle

took its time.

Rate your writing

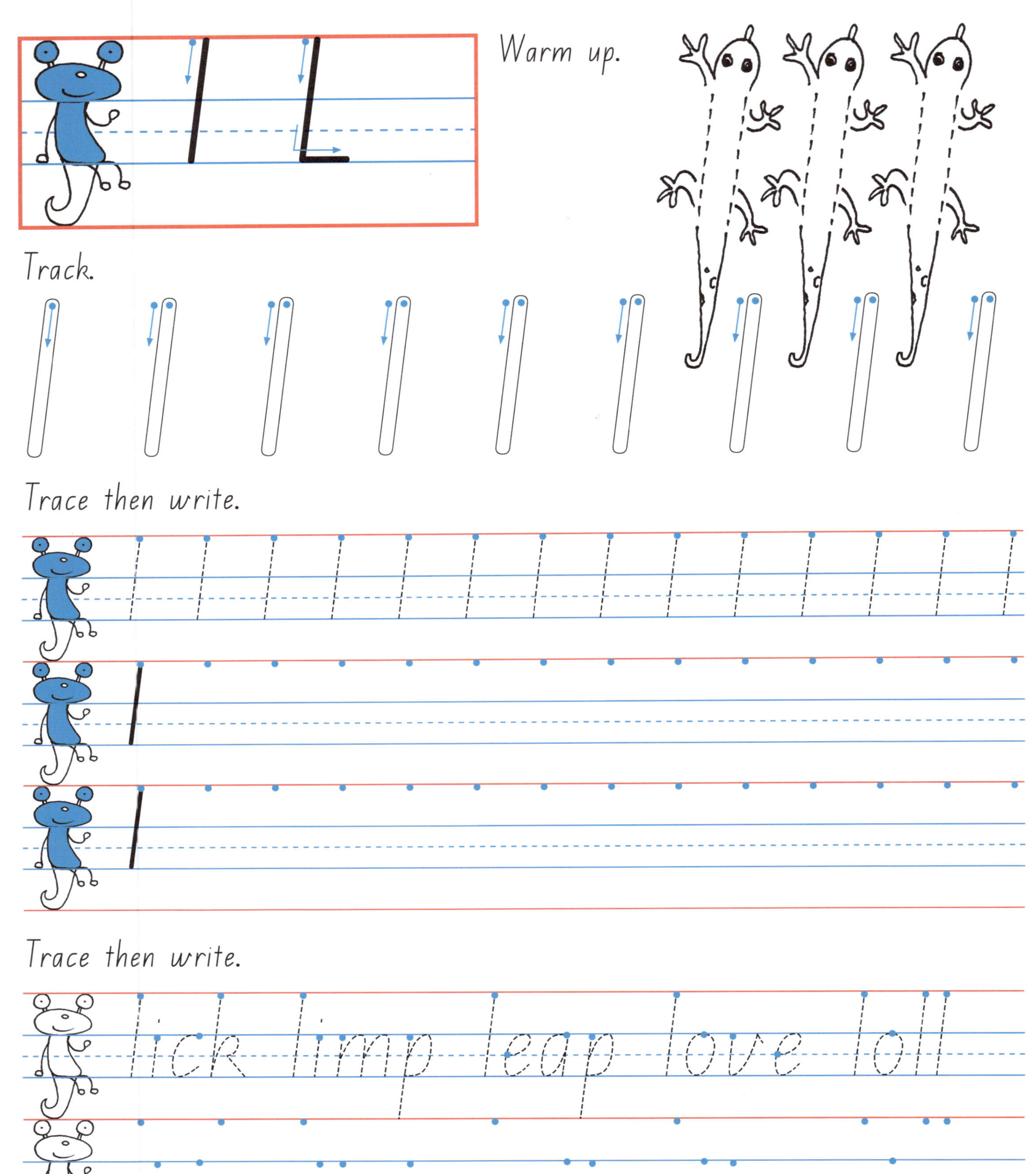

Handwriting: straight-line letter; head and body letter (ascender) (l).
Grammar: simple sentence; proper noun (Lilly); adjective (lovely); action verbs (loll, limp, lick, leap); thinking verbs (loves, love).
Punctuation: upper-case (capital) letter to start a sentence; full stop.
Spelling and vocabulary: lazy, leap, left, lesson, lick, life, lift, limb, limp, lion, list, live, lizard, llama, log, lose, lost, love, lovely, lumpy.
Literary elements: alliteration.

Trace then write.

L L L

l

L

Trace then write.

Little Lilly loves llamas.

Llamas love Lilly too.

Rate your writing

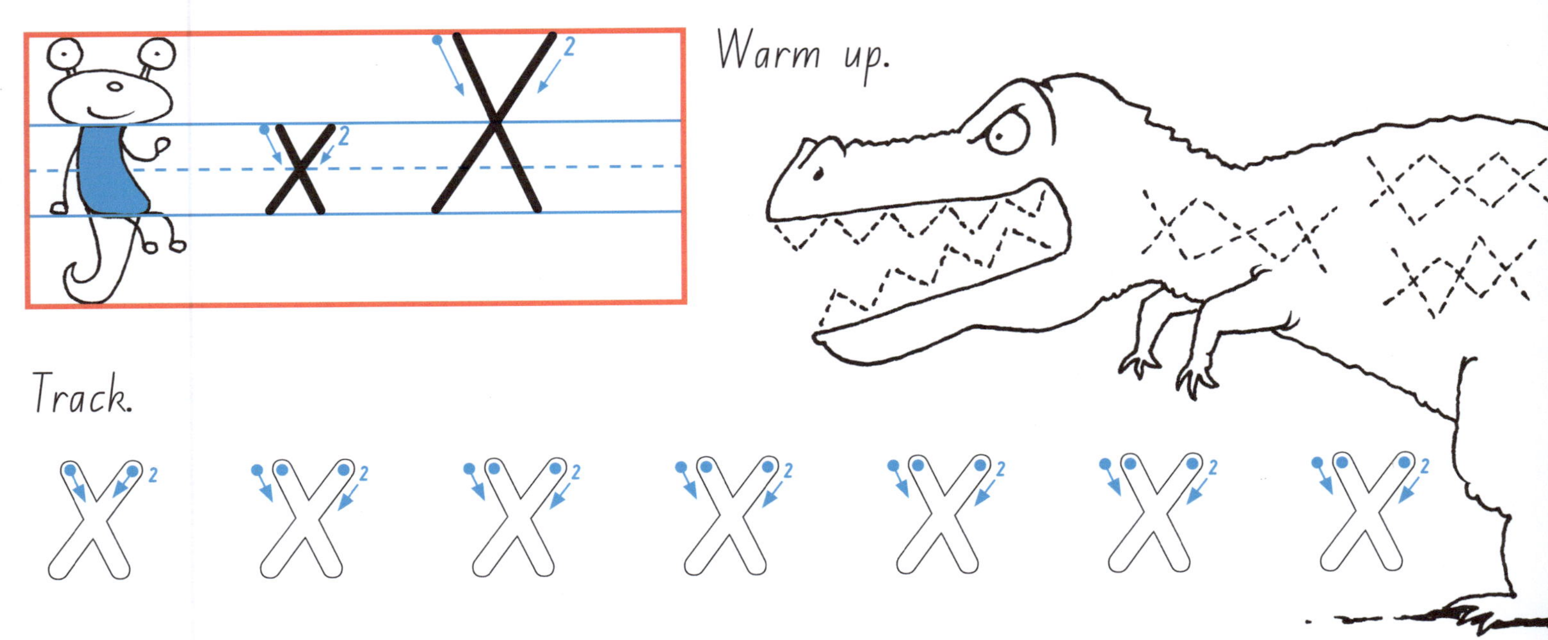

Trace then write.

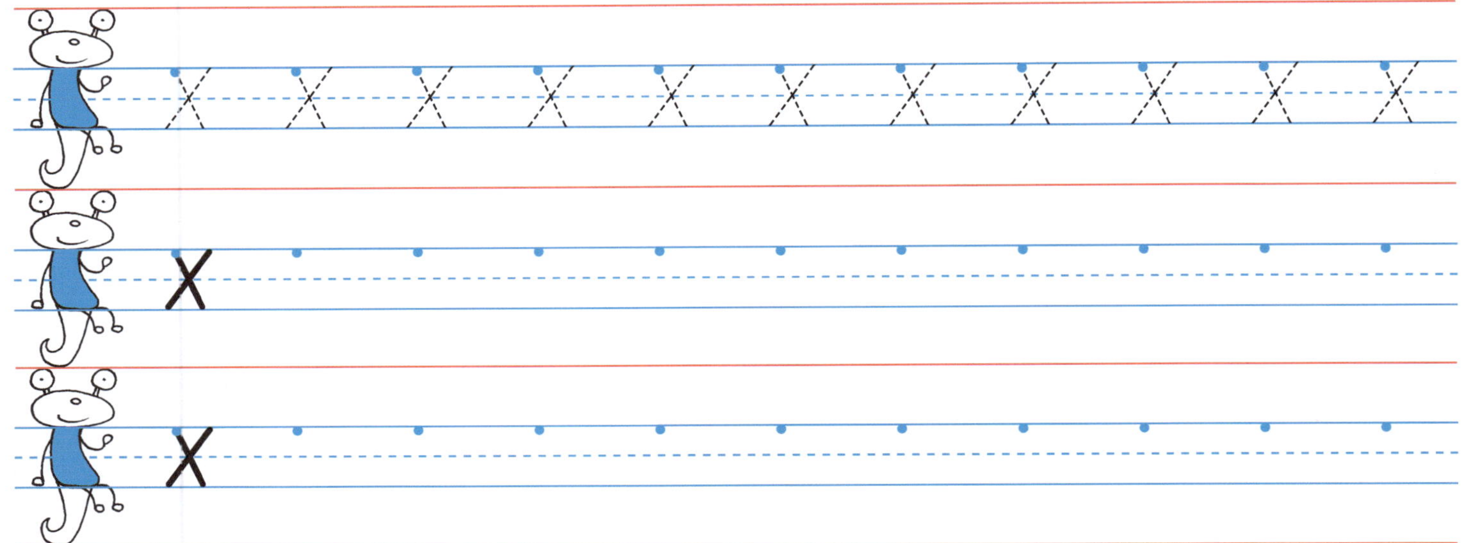

Trace then write.

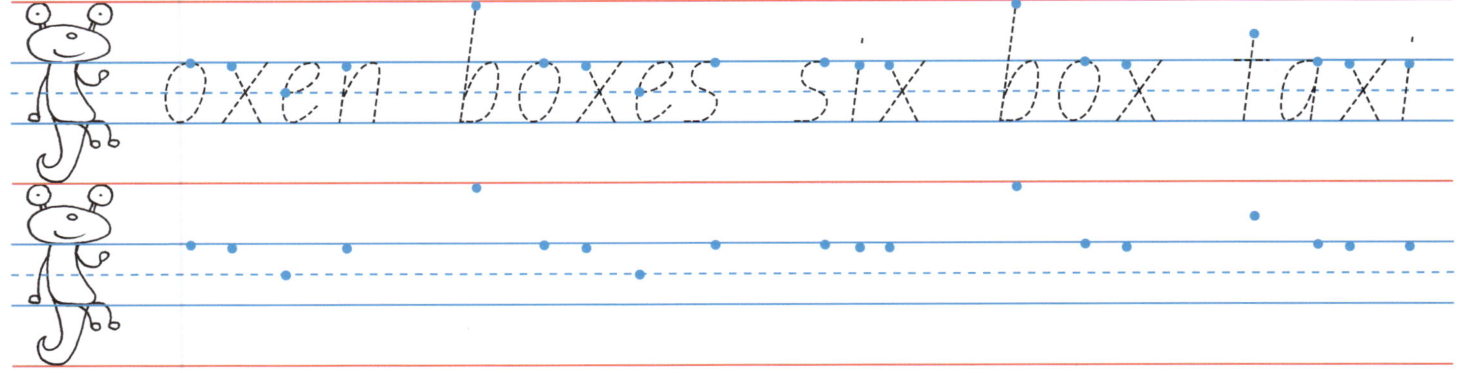

Handwriting: straight-line letter; body letter (x).
Grammar: simple sentence; proper noun (T-Rex); common noun (foxes); saying verb (said); verb group (don't mix); quoted speech.
Punctuation: upper-case (capital) letter to start a sentence; full stop; quotation marks.
Spelling and vocabulary: apostrophe for contraction (don't); box, exam, fox, mix, oxen, six, T-Rex, taxi, text, wax, x-ray, xylophone.
Literary elements: alliteration.

Trace then write.

X X X

x

X

Trace then write.

"Xylophones don't mix

with foxes!" said T-Rex.

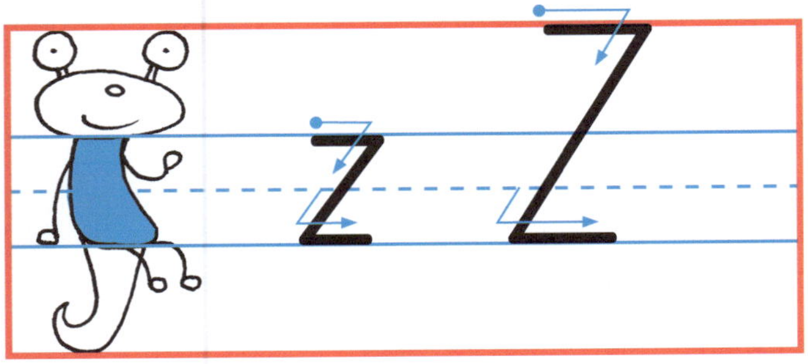

z Z

Warm up.

Track.

Trace then write.

z

Z

Trace then write.

zebra whiz zoo zero

Handwriting: straight-line letter; body letter (z).
Grammar: simple sentence; proper noun (Zoe); possessive apostrophe (Zoe's).
Punctuation: upper-case (capital) letter to start a sentence; full stop.
Spelling and vocabulary: doze, quiz, zany, zap, zebra, zero, zest, zesty, zing, zip, zoo.
Literary elements: alliteration; onomatopoeia (whiz, zip, zap).

Trace then write.

Z Z Z

z

Z

Trace then write.

Zip, zap, zing went

zany Zoe's zither.

Rate your writing

Handwriting: anticlockwise letter; body letter (u).
Grammar: saying verb (uttered); proper noun (Uncle Uno); quoted speech.
Punctuation: upper-case (capital) letter to start a sentence; full stop; exclamation mark; quotation marks.
Spelling and vocabulary: prefix un- (undo, untie, unzip); uncle, under, until, up, upend, upon, umbrella.
Literary elements: alliteration; onomatopoeia (ouch).

Trace then write.

U u U

Ouch!

Trace then write.

Uncle Uno

uttered, "Ouch!"

Rate your writing

Handwriting: anticlockwise letter; body letter (v).
Grammar: simple sentence; proper noun (Vinnie); being verb (was); adjective (vain).
Punctuation: upper-case (capital) letter to start a sentence; full stop.
Spelling and vocabulary: vain, vase, very, vest, vibe, vine, violin, volcano, vole, vote, vow.
Literary elements: alliteration; anthropomorphism; onomatopoeia (vroom).

Trace then write.

V v v

v

V

Trace then write.

Vinnie vole

was very vain.

Rate your writing

Handwriting: anticlockwise letter; body letter (w).
Grammar: saying verb (asked); proper noun (Wally); quoted speech; question.
Punctuation: upper-case (capital) letter to start a sentence; quotation marks; question mark.
Spelling and vocabulary: wall, walrus, watermelon, was, wasp, wave, Wednesday, when, whew, which, whiz, who, wild, wilt, win, wink.
Literary elements: alliteration; anthropomorphism.

Trace then write.

W W W

w

W

Trace then write.

"Who will win?" asked

Wally the walrus.

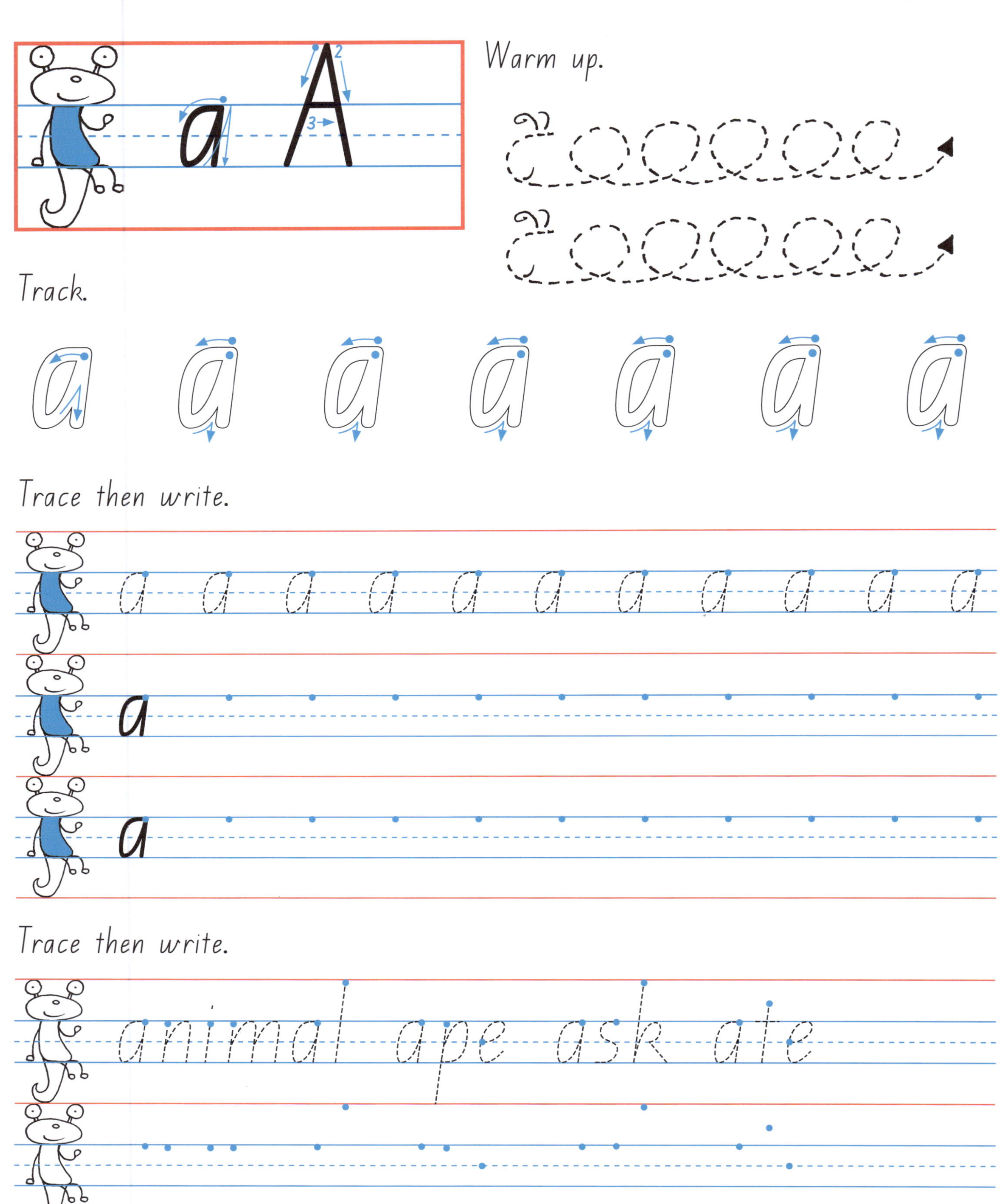

Handwriting: anticlockwise letter; body letter (a).
Grammar: simple sentence; action verb (ate); nouns (anaconda, apples); articles (an, the).
Punctuation: upper-case (capital) letter to start a sentence; full stop.
Spelling and vocabulary: act, again, ago, all, allow, animal, any, ape, apple, April, arm, arrow, ash, ask, ate, August.
Literary elements: alliteration.

Trace then write.

A A A

a

A

Trace then write.

An anaconda ate

all the apples.

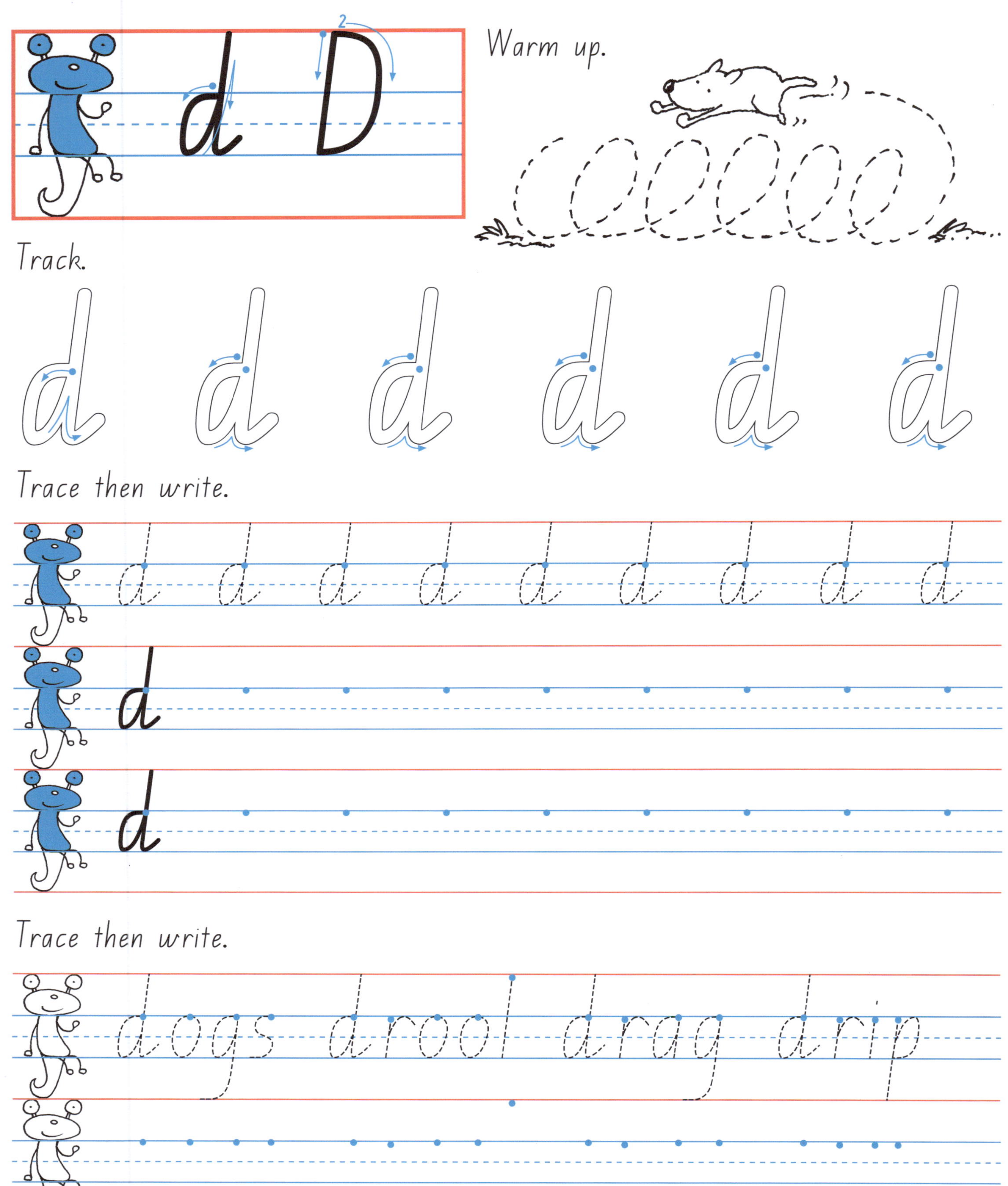

Handwriting: anticlockwise letter; head and body letter (ascender) (d); d has an upward exit to help distinguish it from b.
Grammar: simple sentence; proper noun (Daisy); noun group (daring disco dance).
Punctuation: upper-case (capital) letter to start a sentence; full stop.
Spelling and vocabulary: dance, daring, December, did, disco, do, dog, done, door, drab, drag, drip, drool, drop, drum, doll, duck.
Literary elements: alliteration; anthropomorphism.

Trace then write.

D D D

d

D

Trace then write.

Daisy duck did a

daring disco dance.

Rate your writing

q Q

Warm up.

Track.

q q q q q q q

Trace then write.

q q q q q q q q q q

q

q

Trace then write.

quoll quit quick quiet

Handwriting: anticlockwise letter; body and tail letter (descender) (q).
Grammar: simple sentence; proper noun (Queenie); adjectives (quiet, quick, quicker).
Punctuation: upper-case (capital) letter to start a sentence; full stop.
Spelling and vocabulary: equal, quail, queen, quick, quiet, quit, quite, quiz, quoll.
Literary elements: alliteration.

Trace then write.

Q q Q

Trace then write.

Queenie is quicker

than the quoll.

Rate your writing

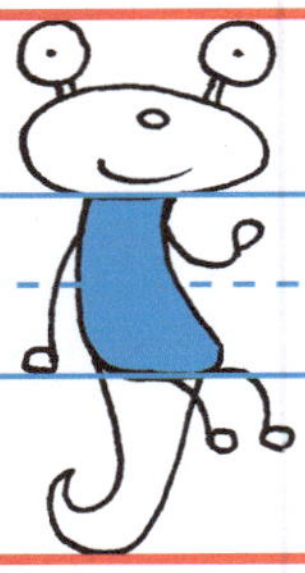

o O

Warm up.

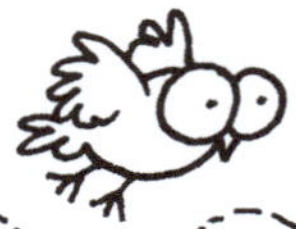

Track.

Trace then write.

Trace then write.

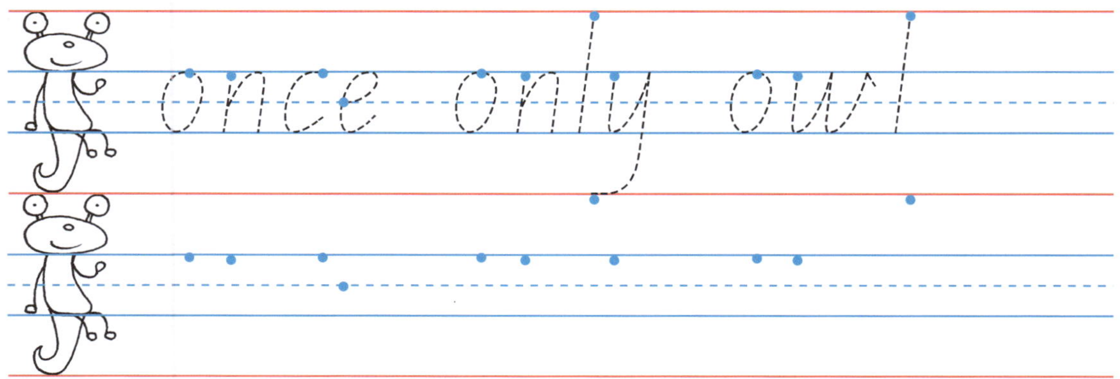

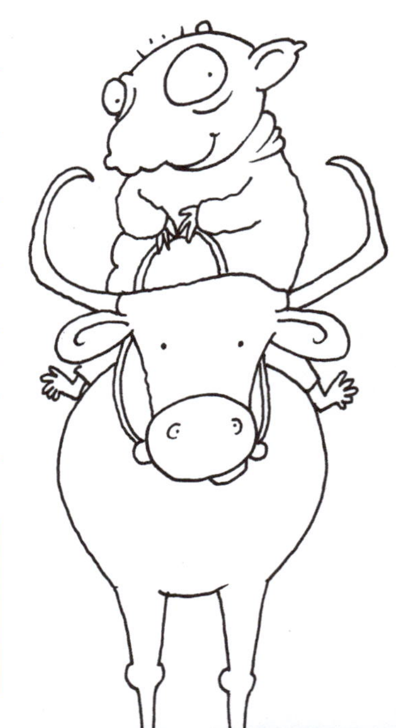

Handwriting: anticlockwise letter; body letter (o).
Grammar: simple sentence; common nouns (ogre, ox); noun groups (One old, orange ogre; the only ox).
Punctuation: upper-case (capital) letter to start a sentence; full stop.
Spelling and vocabulary: October, often, old, once, one, only, open, orange, oven, owl, ox.
Literary elements: alliteration; story character (ogre).

Trace then write.

O O O

o

O

Trace then write.

One old, orange ogre

is on the only ox.

Rate your writing

Handwriting: anticlockwise letter; body letter (e).
Grammar: simple sentence; saying verb (yelled); nouns (eagle, elf) ; noun group (the excited elf); quoted speech.
Punctuation: upper-case (capital) letter to start a sentence; exclamation mark; quotation marks.
Spelling and vocabulary: eagle, ear, earth, eat, eats, eating, egg, elephant, elf, even, every, excited, extra.
Literary elements: alliteration; story characters (elf); onomatopoeia (eek).

Trace then write.

E E E

e

E

Trace then write.

"Eek! An eagle!" yelled

the excited elf.

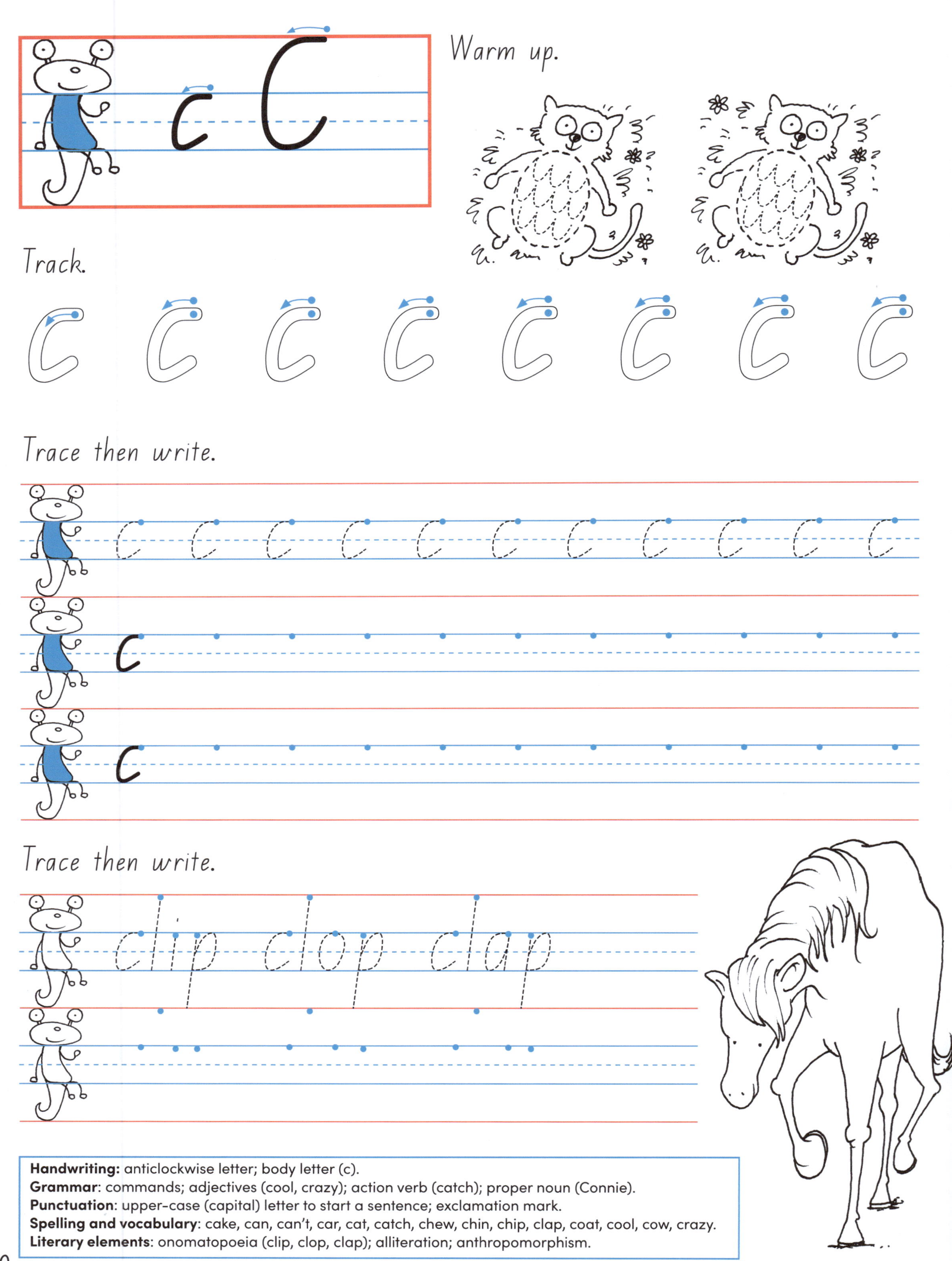

Handwriting: anticlockwise letter; body letter (c).
Grammar: commands; adjectives (cool, crazy); action verb (catch); proper noun (Connie).
Punctuation: upper-case (capital) letter to start a sentence; exclamation mark.
Spelling and vocabulary: cake, can, can't, car, cat, catch, chew, chin, chip, clap, coat, cool, cow, crazy.
Literary elements: onomatopoeia (clip, clop, clap); alliteration; anthropomorphism.

Trace then write.

C C C

c

C

Trace then write.

Catch that crazy,

cool cow, Connie!

Rate your writing

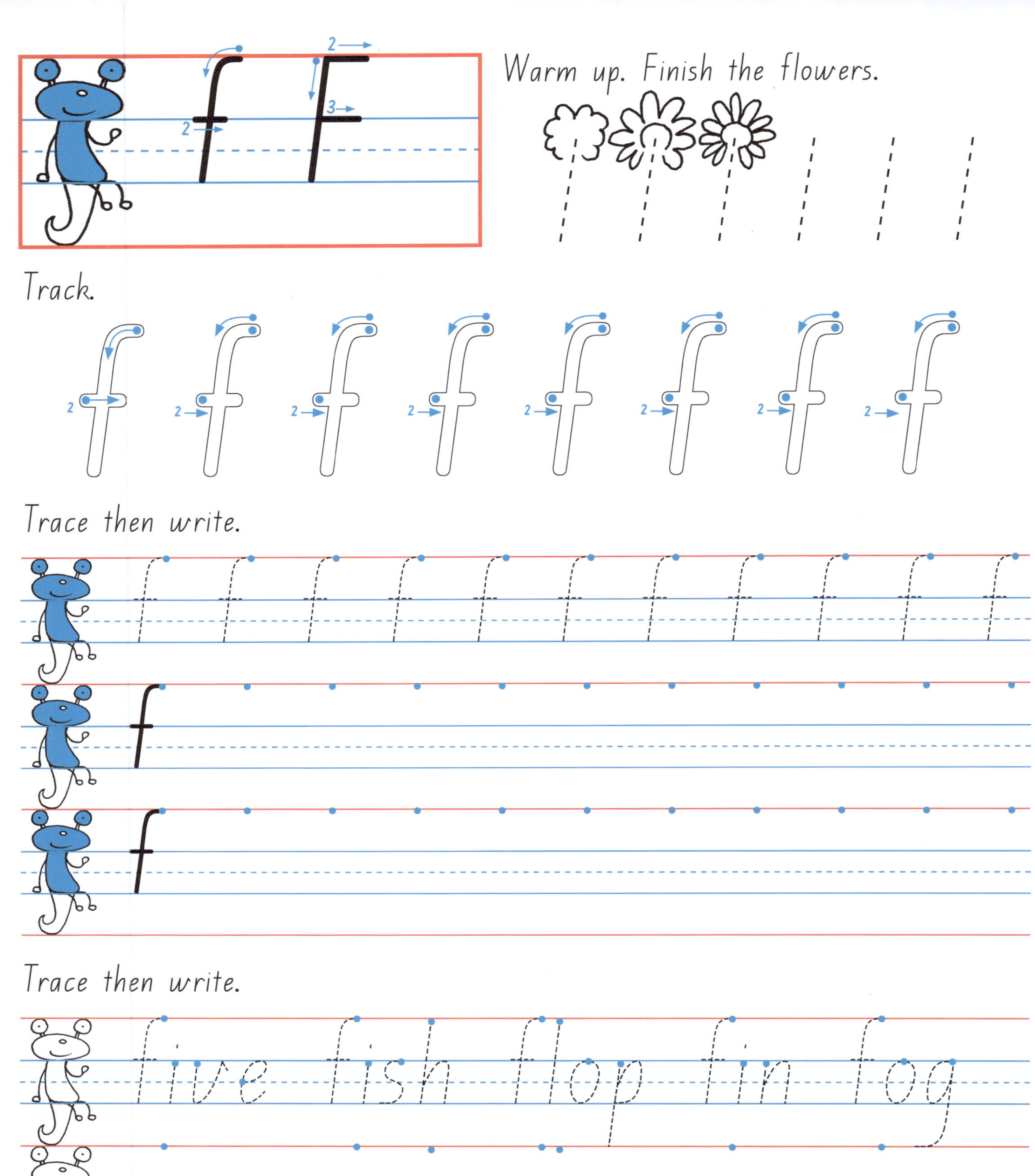

Handwriting: anticlockwise letter; head and body letter (ascender) (f).
Grammar: simple sentence; proper noun (Felix); adjective (fast); action verb (fled); nouns (frog, foot).
Punctuation: upper-case (capital) letter to start a sentence; full stop.
Spelling and vocabulary: fast, February, feel, fin, find, first, fish, fit, five, fled, flesh, flop, foam, fog, foot, Friday, frisky, frog, fry, fun.
Literary elements: alliteration.

Trace then write.
F
f
F
Trace then write.
Fast Felix fled on
foot from the frog.
Rate your writing

Handwriting: direction change letter; body and tail letter (descender) (g). **Grammar**: commands; proper nouns (Gruff, Billy); common noun (bridge); prepositional phrase (off the bridge); saying verb (gasped); quoted speech. **Punctuation**: upper-case (capital) letter to start a sentence; full stop; quotation marks; exclamation mark. **Spelling and vocabulary**: game, get, glue, go, goat, goblin, going, gone, grab, grandma, grandpa, grip, gasped. **Literary elements**: alliteration; folk tale (The Three Billy Goats Gruff); story characters; onomatopoeia (glug).

Trace then write.

G G G

g

G

Trace then write.

"Gruff, get off the

bridge!" gasped Billy.

y Y

Warm up.

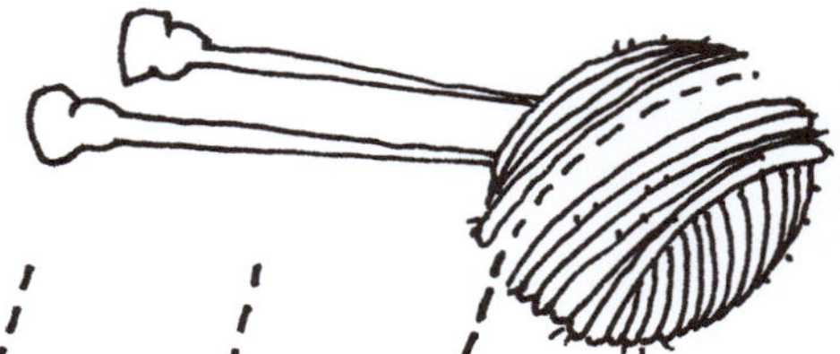

Track.

y y y y y y y

Trace then write.

y y y y y y y y y y y

y

y

Trace then write.

year yawn yes you

Handwriting: direction change letter; body and tail letter (descender) (y).
Grammar: saying verb (yak); nouns (yaks, mats); personal pronoun (you); prepositional phrase (on yoga mats).
Punctuation: upper-case (capital) letter to start a sentence; full stop; speech bubble.
Spelling and vocabulary: yacht, yak, yap, yard, yarn, yawn, year, yen, yep, yes, yeti, yoga, yolk, you, yuan, yummy.
Literary elements: alliteration; onomatopoeia (yakkity yak); anthropomorphism.

Trace then write.

Y Y Y

y

Y

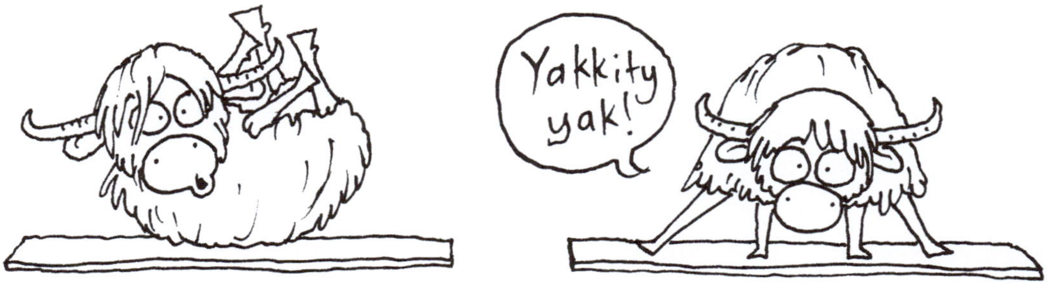

Trace then write.

Yaks yakkity yak

on yoga mats.

Rate your writing

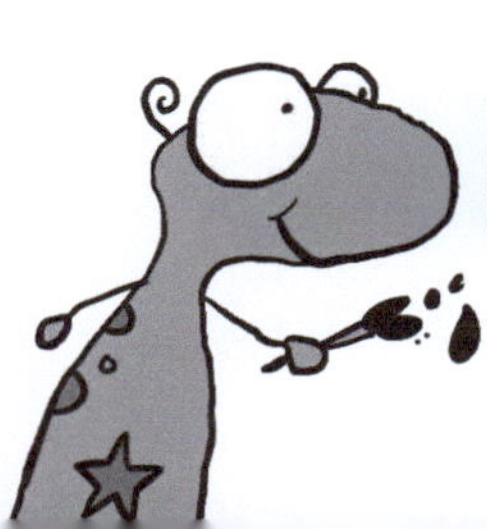

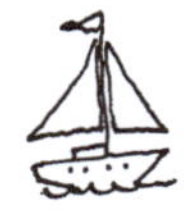

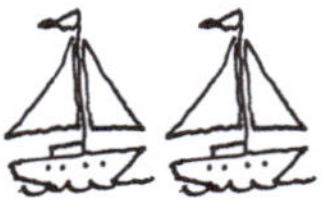

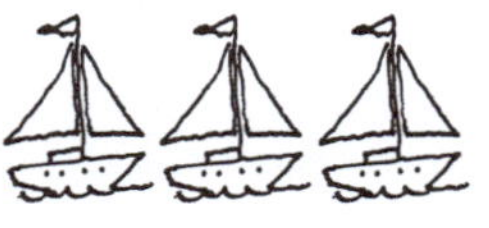

Handwriting: direction change letter; body letter (s).
Grammar: simple sentence; proper noun (Samson); action verb (sat); saying verb (said); noun group (a startled spider).
Punctuation: upper-case (capital) letter to start a sentence; full stop.
Spelling and vocabulary: said, sand, Saturday, saw, see, send, September, seven, sister, six, snail, snort, spider, squid, startled.
Literary elements: alliteration; onomatopoeia (snort).

Trace then write.

S S S

s

S

Trace then write.

Samson almost sat

on a startled spider.

Rate your writing

Trace then write.

1 one

2 two

3 three

4 four

5 five

6 six

7 seven

Rate your writing

☆ ☆☆ ☆☆☆

Trace then write.

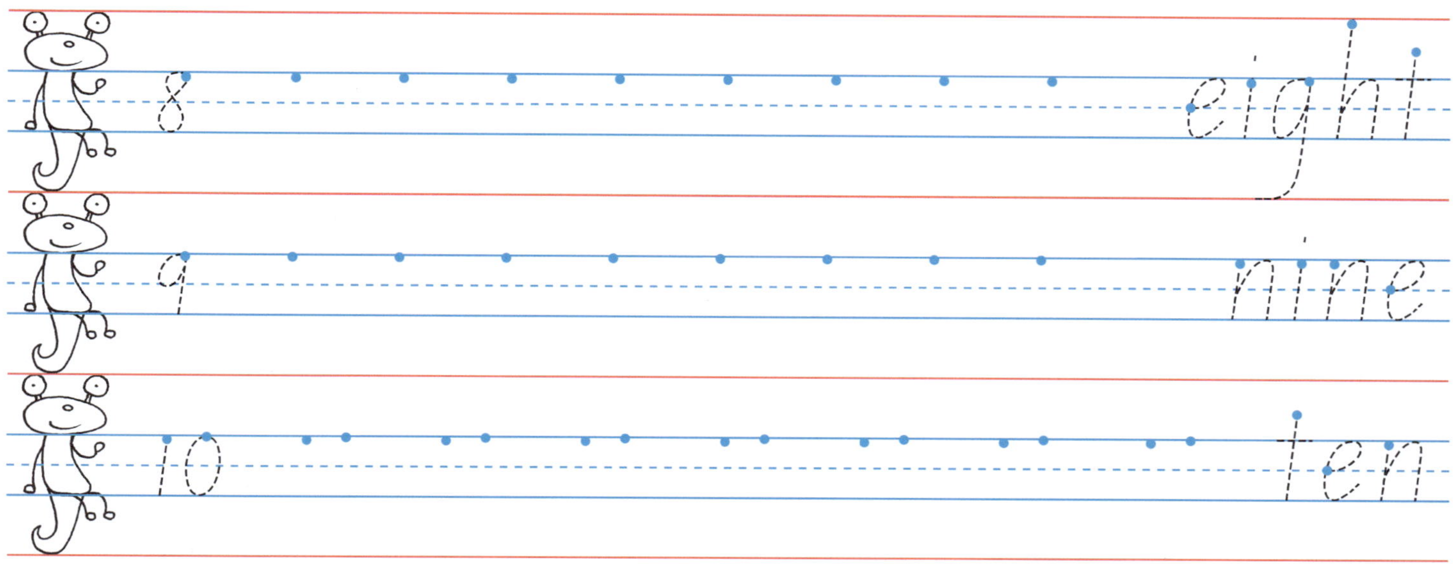

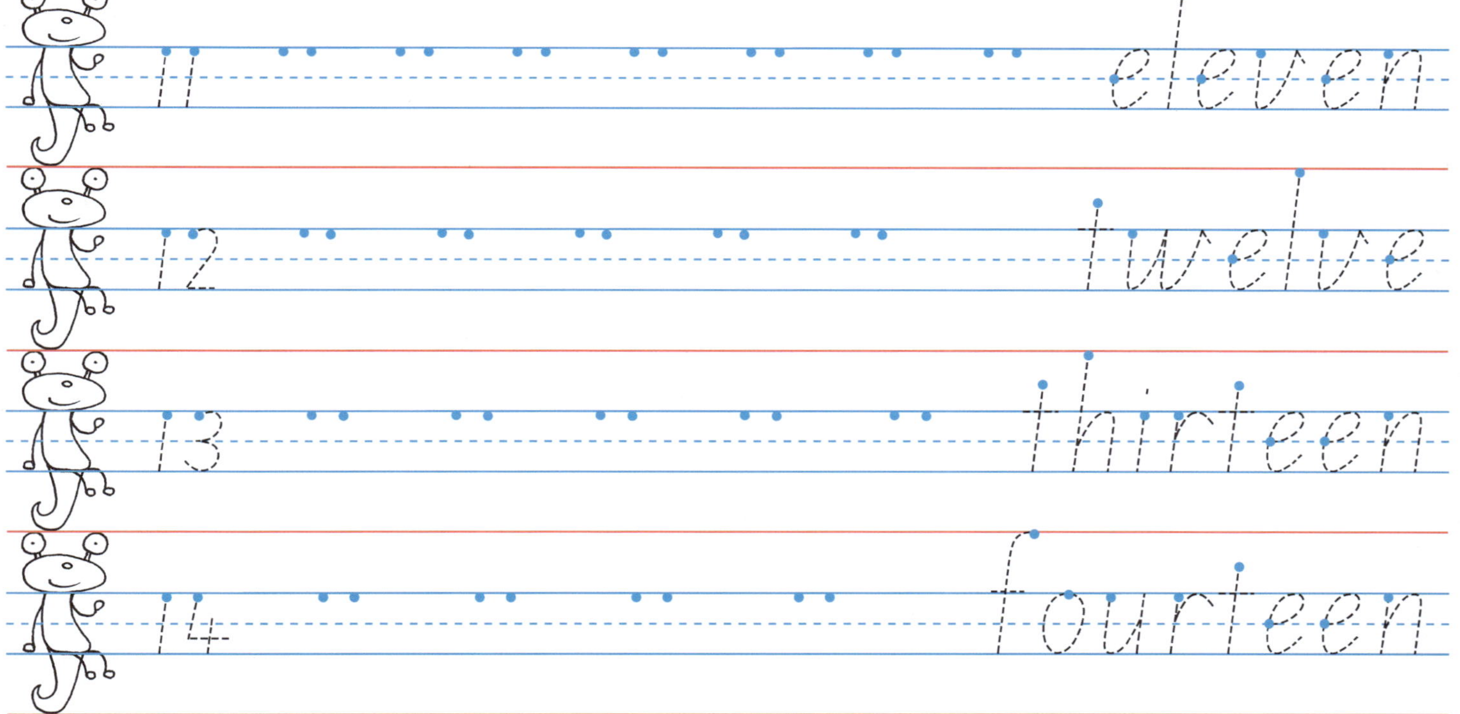

☆ ☆☆ ☆☆☆

Trace then write.

15 fifteen

16 sixteen

17 seventeen

18 eighteen

19 nineteen

20 twenty

30 thirty

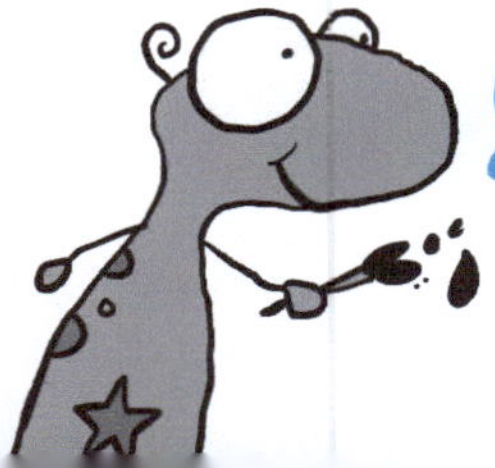

Trace then write.

40 forty

50 fifty

In dog years, she's the same age as me.

60 sixty

70 seventy

80 eighty

90 ninety

100 one hundred

Trace then write.

Trace.